A CURIOUS COLLECTION

OF

OCEAN LIFE

and other Watery Wonders

Sandy Creek
NEW YORK

An Imprint of Sterling Publishing Co., Inc.
1166 Avenue of the Americas
New York, NY 10036

Text © 2016 by Marshall Editions
Illustrations © 2016 by Marshall Editions

Text by Nancy Dickmann

ISBN: 978-1-4351-6572-4

Manufactured in Guangdong, China
Lot #:
4 6 8 10 9 7 5 3
03/19

www.sterlingpublishing.com

A CURIOUS COLLECTION

OF
OCEAN LIFE
and other Watery Wonders

Sandy Creek
NEW YORK

Under the Sea

Oceans cover a huge area of our planet's surface, and when it comes to exploring them, we have really only just scratched the surface. The deeper you go, the darker and more dangerous it gets. Humans need special tools to travel deep and learn about the creatures who live there.

Luckily, sea creatures don't have the same problem! They come in all shapes and sizes, and many of them have special adaptations that help them thrive in different habitats, from colorful coral reefs to the cold, dark ocean floor.

THREE-SPINE
STICKLEBACK

SHANNY

PARTS OF A FISH

TAIL

EYES

BLUE
WHITING

GILLS

FINS

Fish can look very different, but most of them have similar parts. They have gills to take oxygen from the water, and fins and tails to help them swim.

SARDINE

LONGFIN
INSHORE SQUID

Not Just Fish!

Many other creatures also live in the
sea, including mammals and reptiles.
There are also invertebrates of all
shapes and sizes, from tiny shellfish
and crabs to enormous jellyfish
and squid.

BOX
JELLYFISH

BLUEBANDED
SEA SNAKE

ATLANTIC BOTTLE-NOSED
DOLPHIN

HERMIT CRAB

The deep-sea shrimp's
long antennae
help it find food in
the dark.

Ocean Layers

Many fish live near the ocean's surface,
where there is plenty of light and food.
But some creatures have special features
that help them live in the deepest parts
of the ocean, where it is
cold and dark.

DEEP-SEA SHRIMP

LONGLURE
FROGFISH

PHOTOBLEPHARON PALPEBRATUS

Fast Swimmers

Some ocean creatures have a real need for speed. It helps them hunt and makes them hard to catch!

MAKO SHARK

Mako sharks hunt fish such as mackerel and tuna near the surface.

HOUNDFISH

TARPON

SKIPJACK TUNA

The skipjack tuna gets its name because, when it chases its prey at top speed, it appears to "skip" over the ocean's surface.

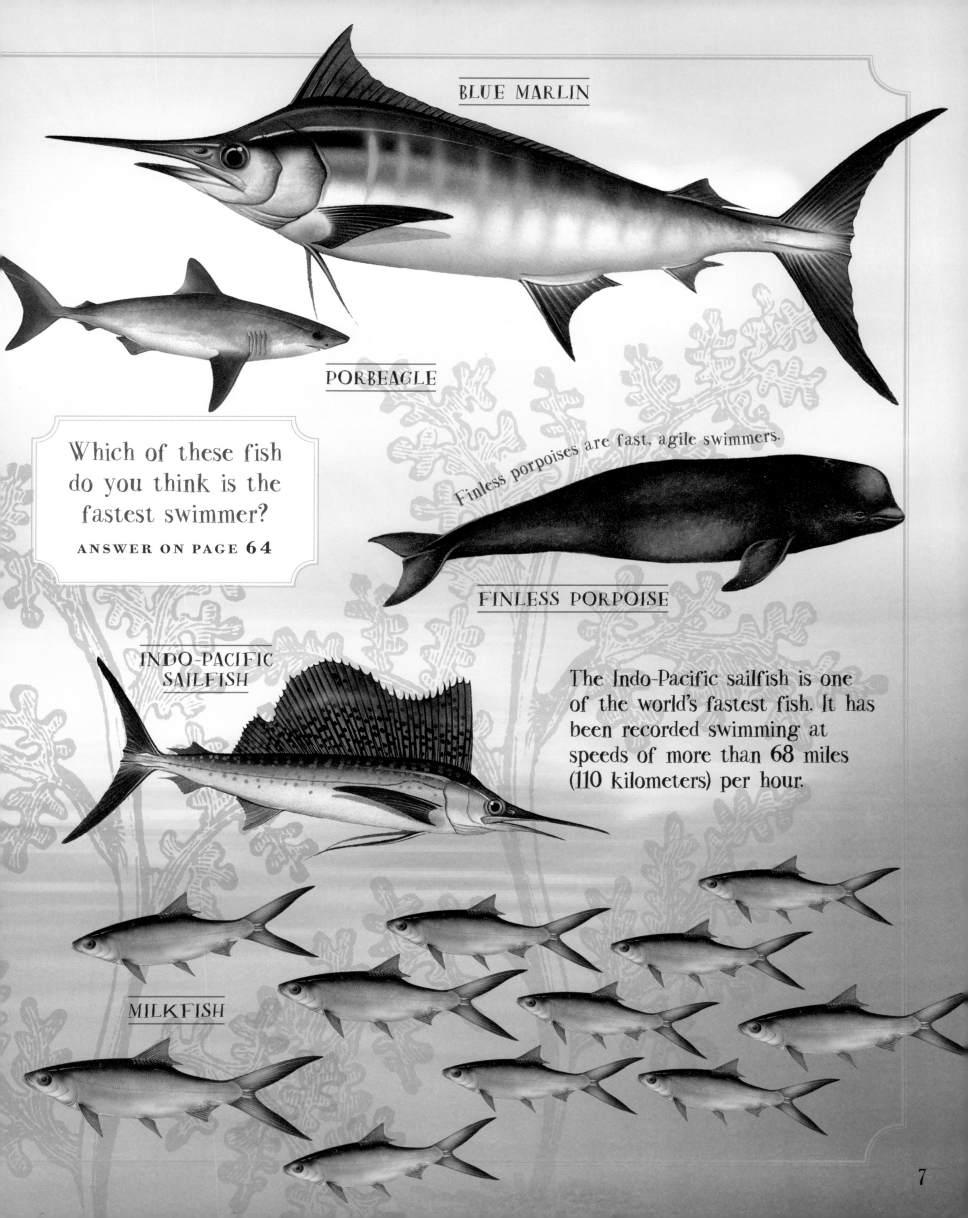

BLUE MARLIN

PORBEAGLE

Which of these fish do you think is the fastest swimmer?

ANSWER ON PAGE 64

Finless porpoises are fast, agile swimmers.

FINLESS PORPOISE

INDO-PACIFIC SAILFISH

The Indo-Pacific sailfish is one of the world's fastest fish. It has been recorded swimming at speeds of more than 68 miles (110 kilometers) per hour.

MILKFISH

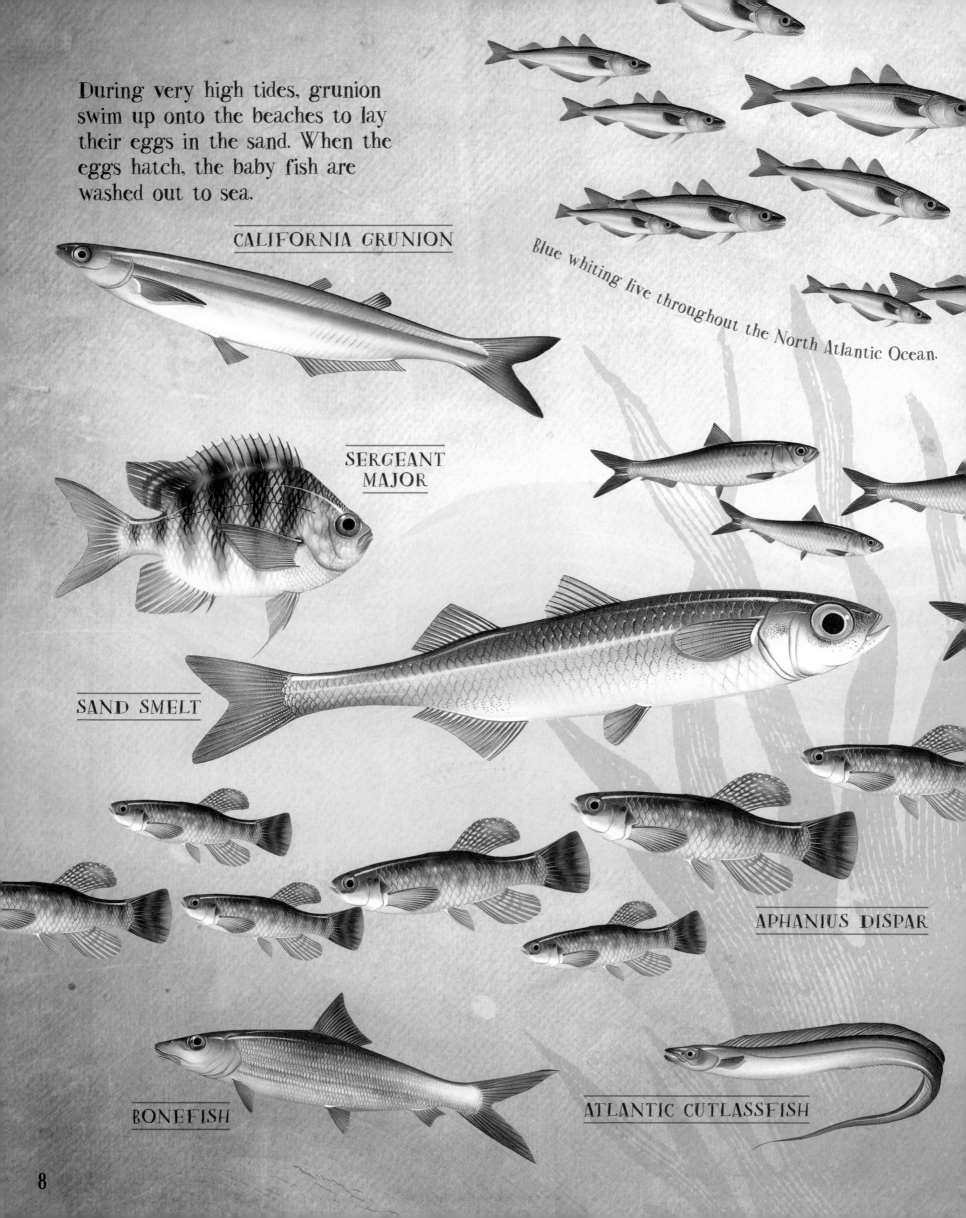

During very high tides, grunion swim up onto the beaches to lay their eggs in the sand. When the eggs hatch, the baby fish are washed out to sea.

CALIFORNIA GRUNION

Blue whiting live throughout the North Atlantic Ocean.

SERGEANT MAJOR

SAND SMELT

APHANIUS DISPAR

BONEFISH

ATLANTIC CUTLASSFISH

8

BLUE PARROTFISH

Blue parrotfish use their "beaks" to scrape algae off of rocks to eat. If they eat any rock, teeth in their throats grind it into sand.

BLUE WHITING

SARDINE

When sardines migrate, they can travel in shoals of millions of fish.

Metallic Beauties
Silvery fish can glint like jewels as they slip and dart through the water.

ATLANTIC HERRING

RED MULLET

GRAY SEAL

Gray seals were nearly hunted to extinction, but now they are a common sight on the eastern coast of Canada, as well as the coasts of northern Europe.

Covered in Spots

Whether they're for camouflage or standing out, these creatures' spots make them unique.

Dolphinfish hunt fish, squid, and crustaceans.

DOLPHINFISH

BLACKCHEEK TONGUEFISH

CLOWN TRIGGERFISH

SARGASSUM TRIGGERFISH

PEACOCK FLOUNDER

HORN SHARK

Horn sharks get their name because of the sharp spines, or "horns," in front of the fins on their backs.

SANDY DOGFISH

MAN-OF-WAR FISH

WINDOWPANE

CALIFORNIA FLOUNDER

MORAY EEL

BANDTAIL PUFFER

A sand tiger's fierce-looking teeth point in all directions.

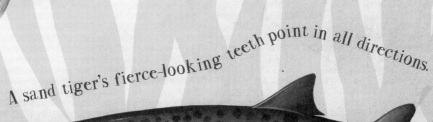

SAND TIGER

11

Shells

Soft-bodied sea creatures often have hard, beautiful shells to protect themselves.

LAMP SHELL

MUSSEL

NAUTILUS

EDIBLE CRAB

HERMIT CRAB

Green turtles graze on sea grasses and algae.

GREEN TURTLE

A hermit crab has no hard shell of its own, so it finds another creature's discarded shell to use. When the crab gets too big, it finds a bigger shell.

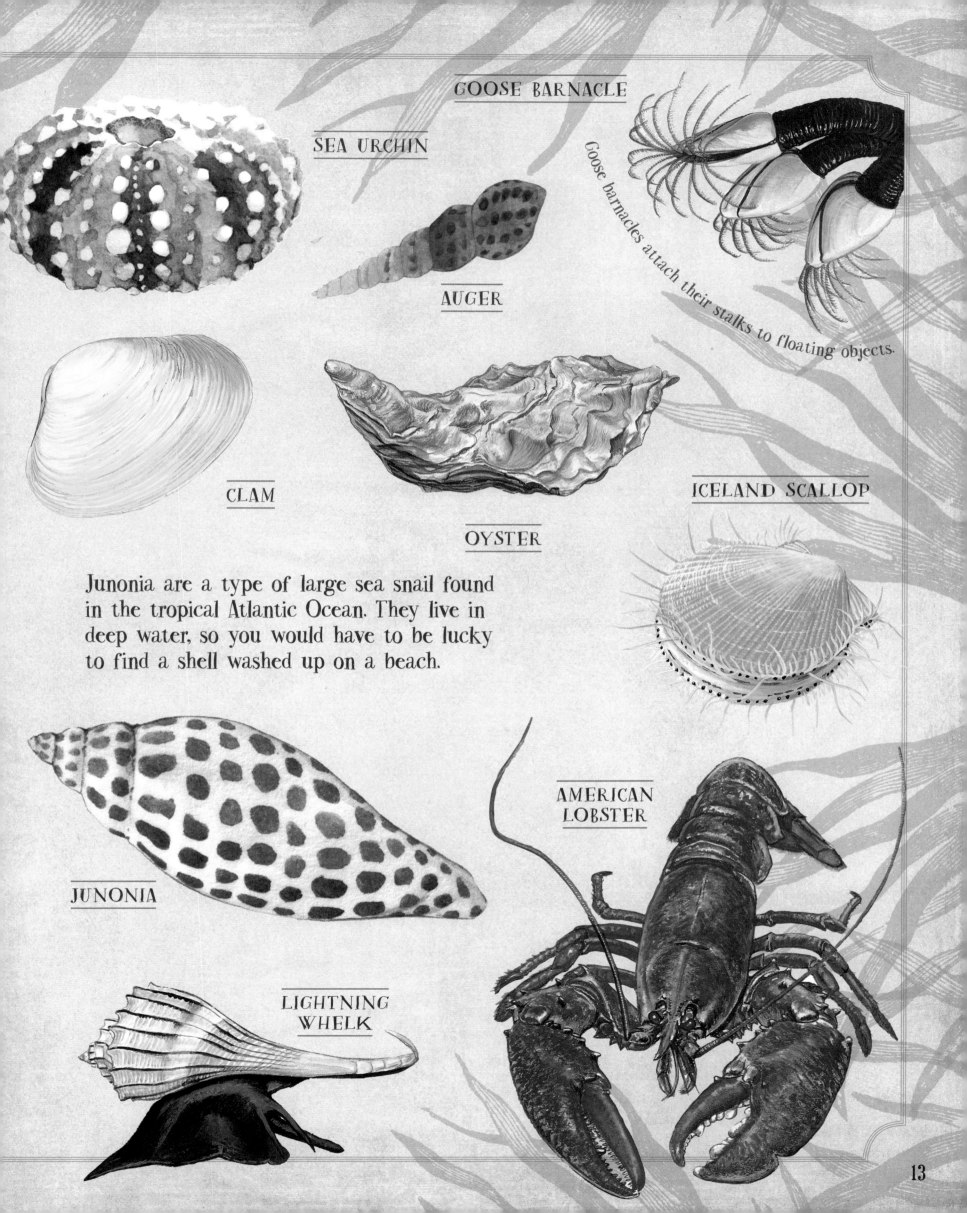

GOOSE BARNACLE

SEA URCHIN

Goose barnacles attach their stalks to floating objects.

AUGER

CLAM

OYSTER

ICELAND SCALLOP

Junonia are a type of large sea snail found in the tropical Atlantic Ocean. They live in deep water, so you would have to be lucky to find a shell washed up on a beach.

JUNONIA

AMERICAN LOBSTER

LIGHTNING WHELK

Squishy and Slimy

Sea creatures come in all different shapes—and some shapes are a little bit weird!

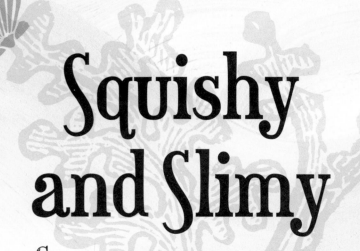

CHROMODORIS NUDIBRANCH

This deep-sea fish has a soft, fragile body.

ATELOPUS JAPONICUS

OCEAN POUT

COMMON COMB JELLY

BEROE COMB JELLY

MAUVE STINGER

Although comb jellies' bodies are made of a jelly-like substance, they are not jellyfish. They have "combs" made up of tiny hairs that they use to paddle through the water.

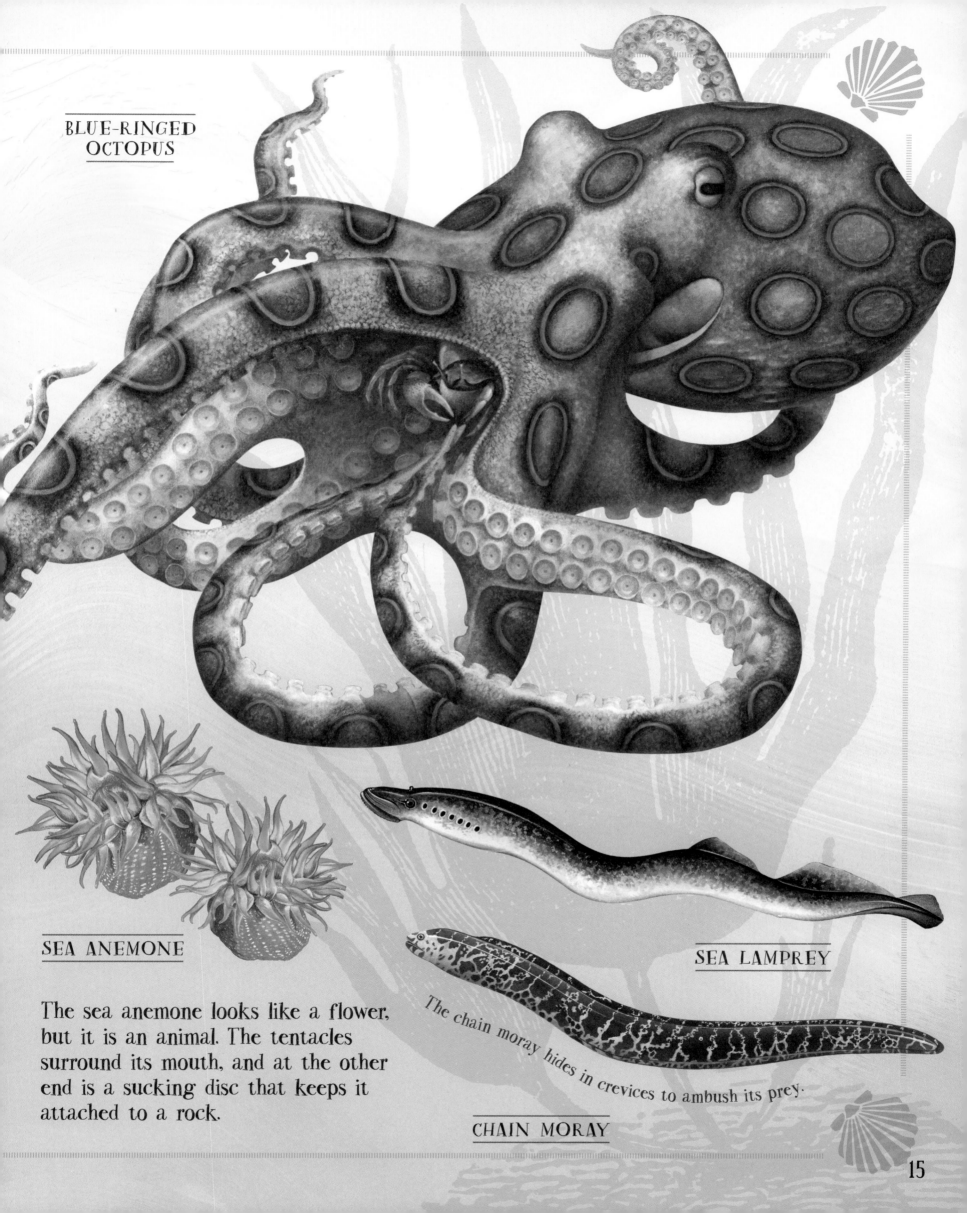

BLUE-RINGED OCTOPUS

SEA ANEMONE

SEA LAMPREY

The sea anemone looks like a flower, but it is an animal. The tentacles surround its mouth, and at the other end is a sucking disc that keeps it attached to a rock.

The chain moray hides in crevices to ambush its prey.

CHAIN MORAY

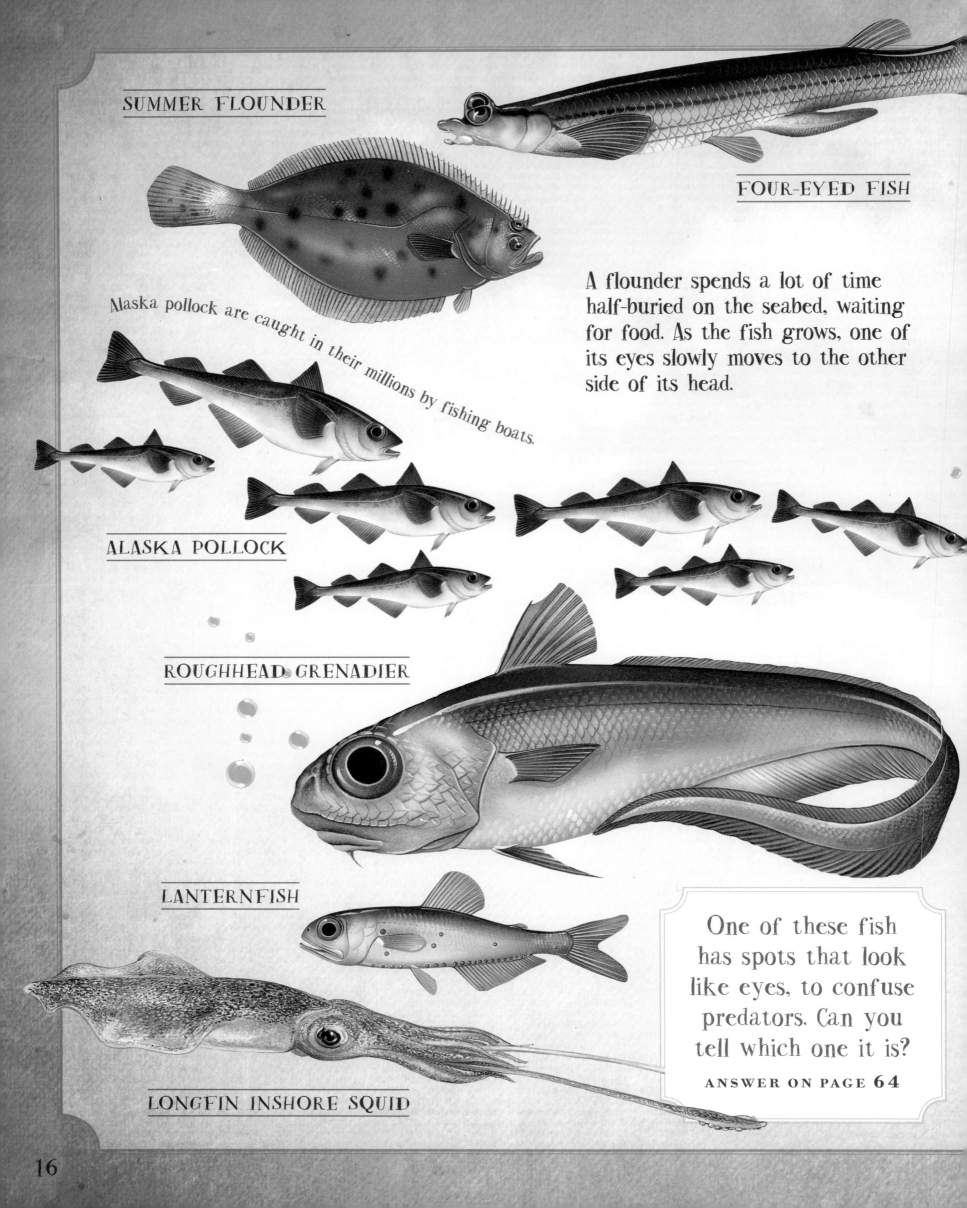

SUMMER FLOUNDER

FOUR-EYED FISH

A flounder spends a lot of time half-buried on the seabed, waiting for food. As the fish grows, one of its eyes slowly moves to the other side of its head.

Alaska pollock are caught in their millions by fishing boats.

ALASKA POLLOCK

ROUGHHEAD GRENADIER

LANTERNFISH

LONGFIN INSHORE SQUID

One of these fish has spots that look like eyes, to confuse predators. Can you tell which one it is?

ANSWER ON PAGE 64

The four-eyed fish actually only has two eyes, each divided into two parts. The top part is for seeing in the air, and the bottom part sees in water.

ANOMALOPS KAPTOPTRON

COPPERBAND BUTTERFLYFISH

The Eyes Have It

The unusual eyes on these fish help them to spot danger and find prey.

Hardhead silversides are tiny: about 3 inches (7.5 centimeters) long.

HARDHEAD SILVERSIDE

RATFISH

HATCHETFISH

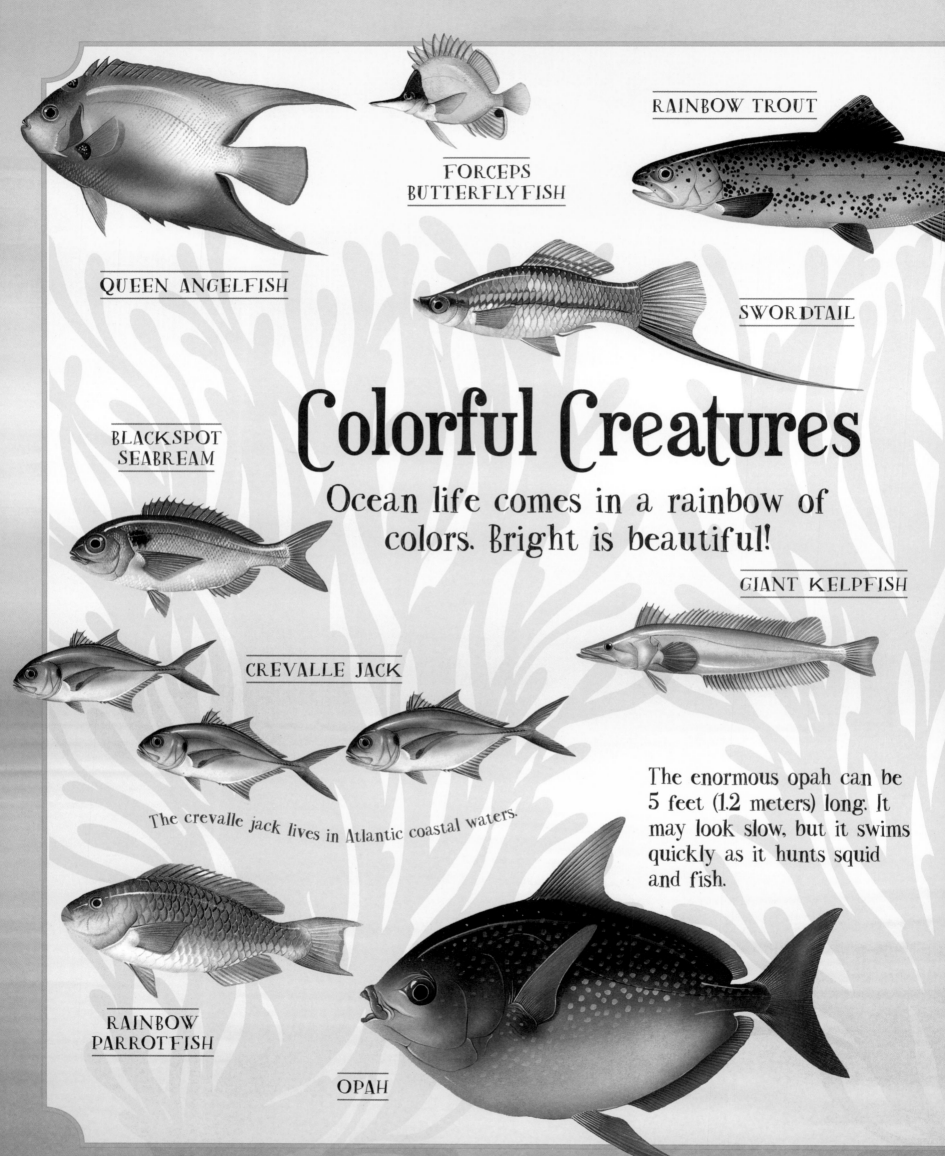

FORCEPS BUTTERFLYFISH

RAINBOW TROUT

QUEEN ANGELFISH

SWORDTAIL

BLACKSPOT SEABREAM

Colorful Creatures

Ocean life comes in a rainbow of colors. Bright is beautiful!

GIANT KELPFISH

CREVALLE JACK

The crevalle jack lives in Atlantic coastal waters.

The enormous opah can be 5 feet (1.2 meters) long. It may look slow, but it swims quickly as it hunts squid and fish.

RAINBOW PARROTFISH

OPAH

MUMMICHOG

ORANGE ROUGHY

BLUE TANG

BEAUGREGORY

Why is this blue tang yellow? The young of this species are yellow with blue markings. Their color changes as they grow, and they are completely blue as adults.

REDFISH

SQUIRRELFISH

GREEN PADDLE WORM

Purple sea snails make "rafts" of bubbles to float on the ocean's surface.

PURPLE SEA SNAIL

DALL'S PORPOISE

COMMON DOLPHIN

ATLANTIC BOTTLE-NOSED
DOLPHIN

PYGMY SPERM
WHALE

The pygmy sperm whale is only a fraction of the size of a sperm whale.

SHEPHERD'S BEAKED
WHALE

This rare whale was only
discovered in the 1930s.
It has been spotted off
the coasts of New Zealand,
Chile, and Argentina.

Whales, Dolphins and Porpoises

These mammals may need to come to the surface to breathe, but they are still completely at home in the water.

Gray whales swim from Alaska to Mexico and back again every year.

STRIPED DOLPHIN

GRAY WHALE

The sei whale is one of the biggest and fastest of all whales. Every day it eats about 2,000 pounds (900 kilograms) of squid, fish, and plankton.

SEI WHALE

Lakes and Ponds

Many water creatures
are adapted for life in
freshwater ponds and lakes.

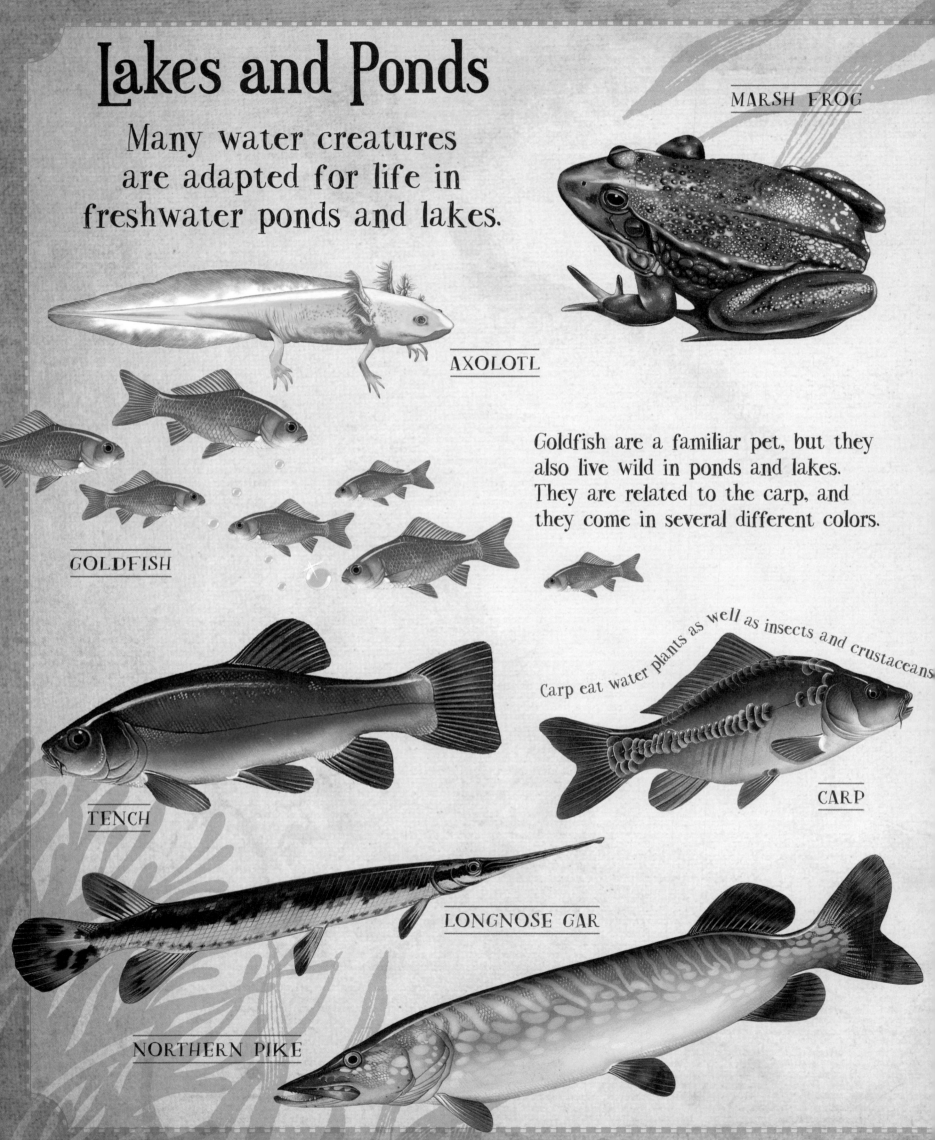

MARSH FROG

AXOLOTL

GOLDFISH

Goldfish are a familiar pet, but they
also live wild in ponds and lakes.
They are related to the carp, and
they come in several different colors.

Carp eat water plants as well as insects and crustaceans

CARP

TENCH

LONGNOSE GAR

NORTHERN PIKE

The false map turtle gets its name because of the lines and blotches on its shell. The markings are brighter on young turtles.

FALSE MAP TURTLE

SPINY SOFT-SHELL

ALLIGATOR SNAPPING TURTLE

A male bowfin guards the female's eggs until they hatch.

BOWFIN

YELLOW-BELLIED SLIDER TURTLE

Can you find the two amphibians on these pages?

ANSWER ON PAGE 64

BICHIR

NILE SOFT-SHELL

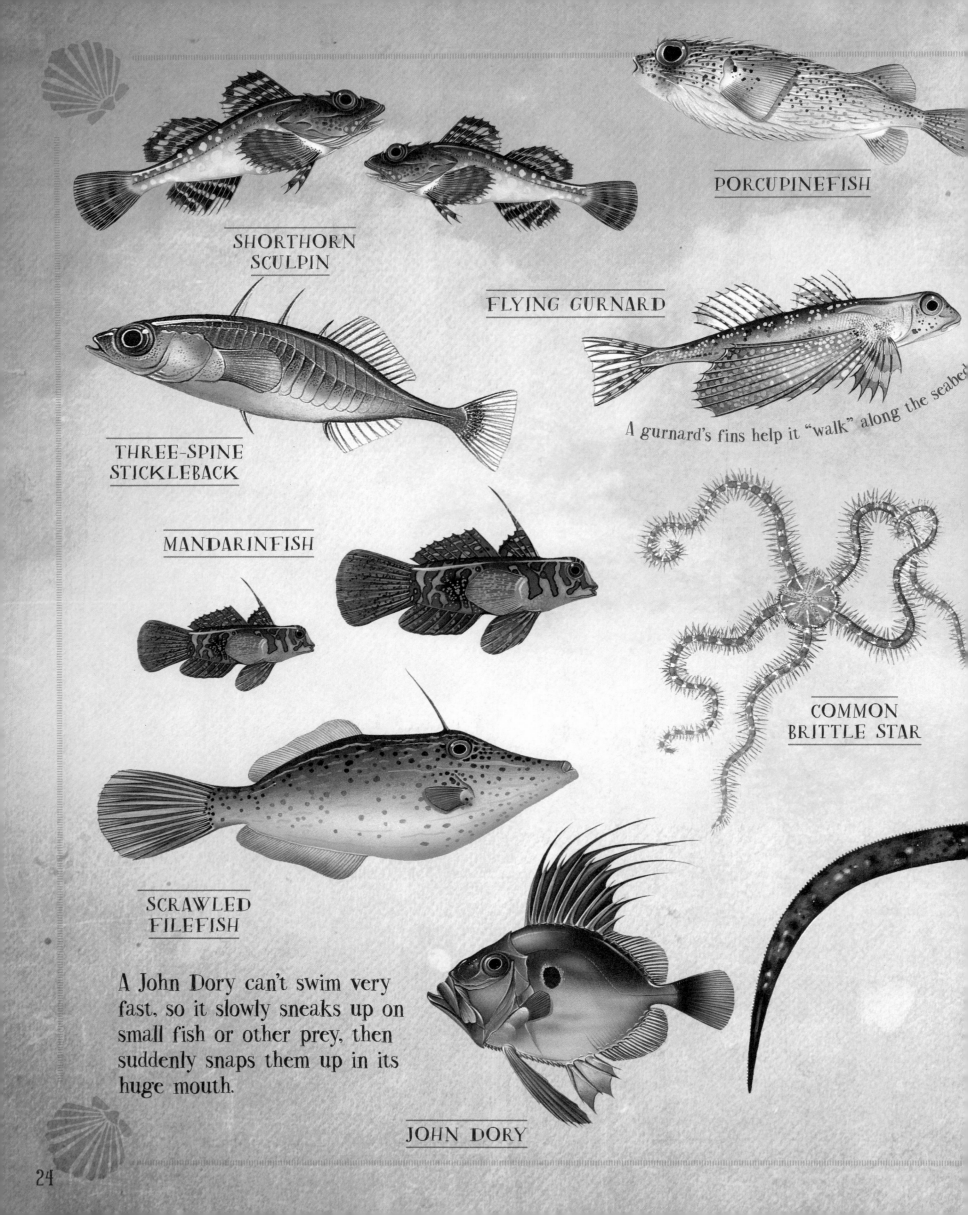

PORCUPINEFISH

SHORTHORN
SCULPIN

FLYING GURNARD

A gurnard's fins help it "walk" along the seabed

THREE-SPINE
STICKLEBACK

MANDARINFISH

COMMON
BRITTLE STAR

SCRAWLED
FILEFISH

A John Dory can't swim very
fast, so it slowly sneaks up on
small fish or other prey, then
suddenly snaps them up in its
huge mouth.

JOHN DORY

Spiny sea stars grow to about 7 inches (18 centimeters) wide. Their backs are covered in rows of short, cone-shaped spines.

ATLANTIC MIDSHIPMAN

SPINY SEA STAR

Spikes and Spines

Bristly, prickly, and sometimes scary, these creatures and their spines aren't messing around.

DRAGONET

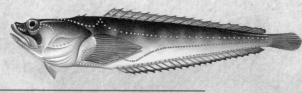

Marine iguanas are the only lizards that live in the sea.

MARINE IGUANA

NORTHERN SEAROBIN

LONG-SPINED URCHIN

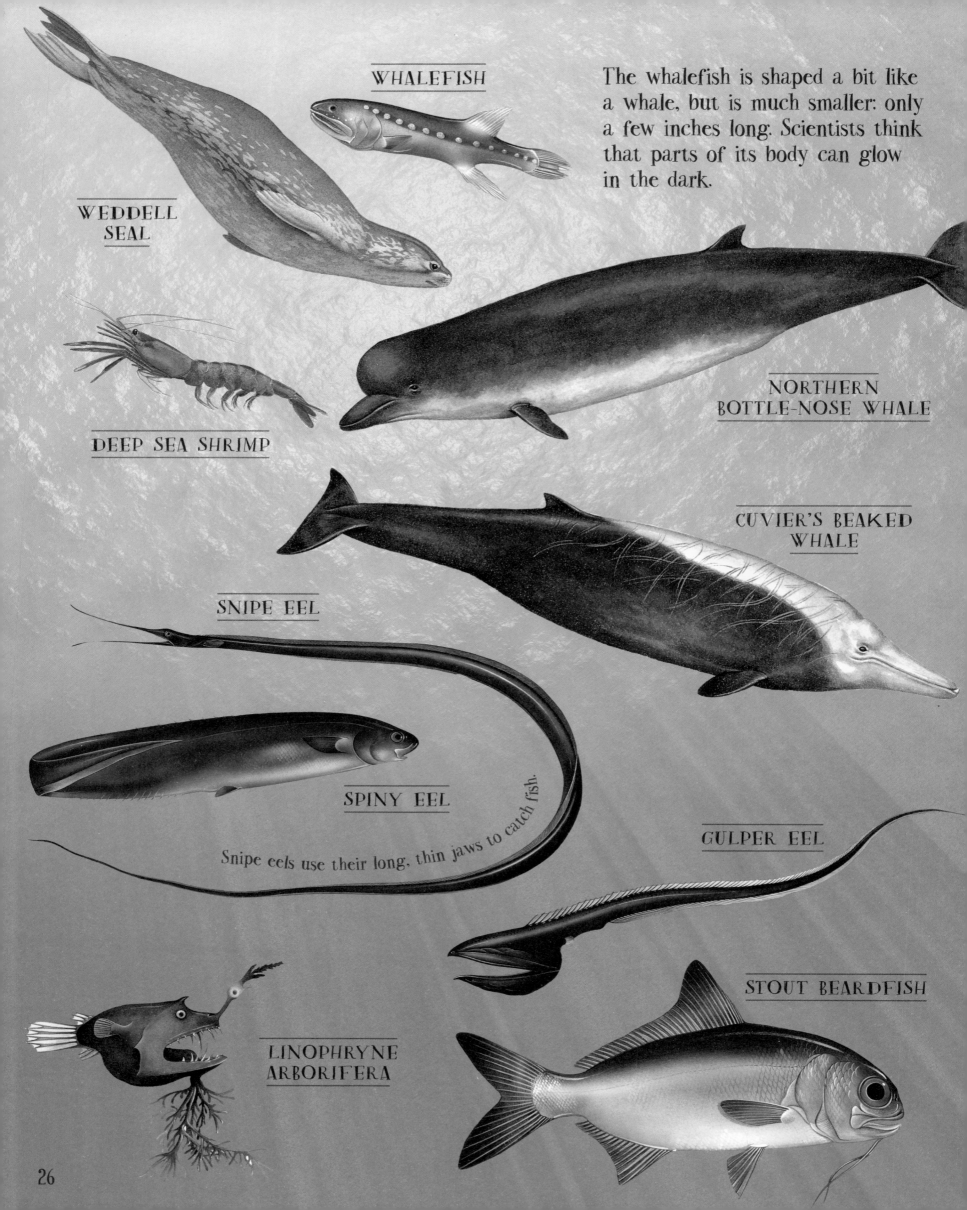

WHALEFISH

The whalefish is shaped a bit like a whale, but is much smaller: only a few inches long. Scientists think that parts of its body can glow in the dark.

WEDDELL SEAL

NORTHERN BOTTLE-NOSE WHALE

DEEP SEA SHRIMP

CUVIER'S BEAKED WHALE

SNIPE EEL

SPINY EEL

Snipe eels use their long, thin jaws to catch fish.

GULPER EEL

STOUT BEARDFISH

LINOPHRYNE ARBORIFERA

26

ATLANTIC FOOTBALLFISH

Deep Sea Monsters

The deepest parts of the ocean are home to an array of weird creatures.

ORANGE ROUGHY

The angler uses the spine on its head as a lure to attract fish to eat.

Viperfish are small, but their teeth are enormous in relation to their size. They can impale their prey by swimming at them with their mouths open.

SLOANE'S VIPERFISH

ANGLER

SEA LILY

SPOTTED LANTERNFISH

GIANT ISOPOD

BATFISH

The redlip blenny is found on reefs throughout the Gulf of Mexico and Caribbean Sea. It is also a popular fish in aquariums.

REDLIP BLENNY

YELLOW BOXFISH

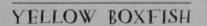
A squirrelfish's large eyes help it see at night, when it is most active.

SQUIRRELFISH

CLOWN ANEMONEFISH

VASE SPONGE

Coral Reefs

Coral reefs provide a habitat for a huge range of fish and other creatures.

WEEDY SEADRAGON

The flaps of skin on this seadragon's body help it stay hidden among the seaweed, protecting it from predators.

STRIPED-FACE UNICORNFISH

ATLANTIC DEER COWRIE

Which of these reef fish has an armored body for protection?

ANSWER ON PAGE 64

Rainbow parrotfish can be 4 feet (1.2 meters) long.

RAINBOW PARROTFISH

QUEEN TRIGGERFISH

MAGNIFICENT FEATHER DUSTER

CONEY

The Biggest Ever

The blue whale is the largest creature that has ever lived on Earth. No matter how you measure it, it's a whopper!

BLUE WHALE

With a length of 105 feet (32 meters), the blue whale is longer than two school buses.

The blue whale is so enormous that you might think it eats large creatures such as sharks or other whales. But it actually eats tiny shrimp-like creatures called krill.

It weighs as much as 40 elephants.

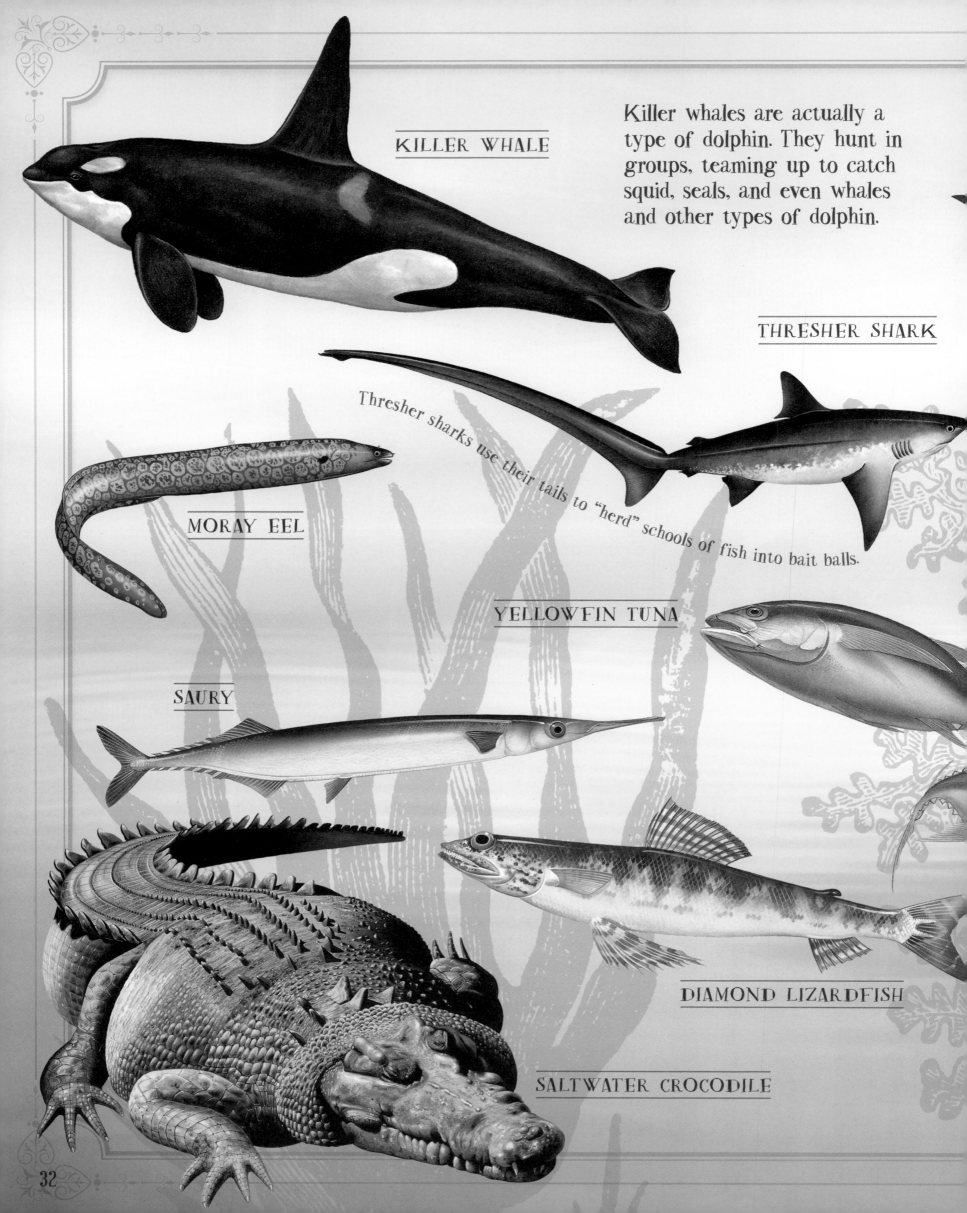

KILLER WHALE

Killer whales are actually a type of dolphin. They hunt in groups, teaming up to catch squid, seals, and even whales and other types of dolphin.

THRESHER SHARK

Thresher sharks use their tails to "herd" schools of fish into bait balls.

MORAY EEL

YELLOWFIN TUNA

SAURY

DIAMOND LIZARDFISH

SALTWATER CROCODILE

GREAT WHITE SHARK

Great white sharks have sometimes been known to attack humans.

SWORDFISH

Fierce Predators

It's a fish-eat-fish world out there, and smaller animals don't stand a chance against these fearsome hunters.

BARRACUDA

Which of these hunters tips seals off of ice floes to catch them?

ANSWER ON PAGE 64

LEOPARD SEAL

Leopard seals live in the waters around Antarctica. They are strong, fast swimmers who hunt penguins, fish, and sometimes even other species of seals.

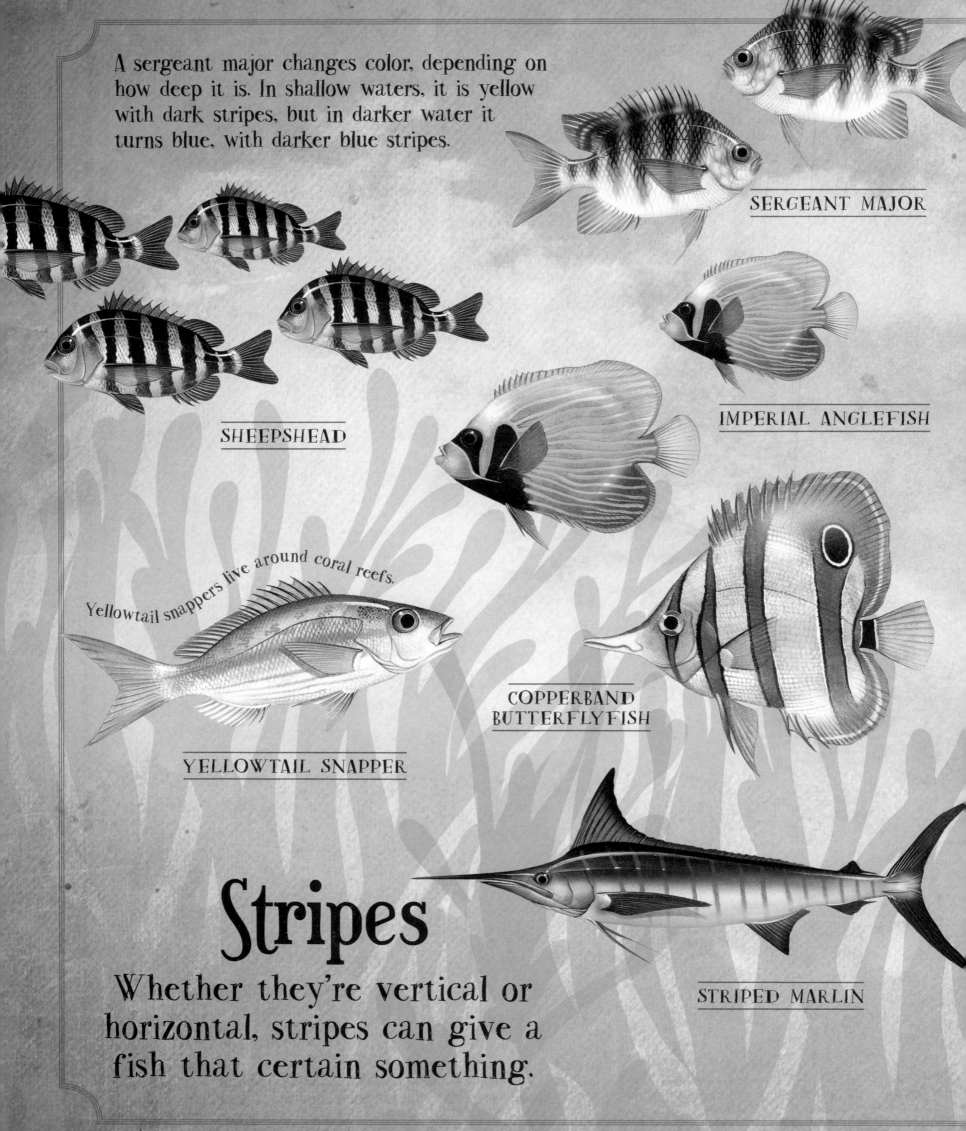

A sergeant major changes color, depending on how deep it is. In shallow waters, it is yellow with dark stripes, but in darker water it turns blue, with darker blue stripes.

SERGEANT MAJOR

SHEEPSHEAD

IMPERIAL ANGLEFISH

Yellowtail snappers live around coral reefs.

COPPERBAND BUTTERFLYFISH

YELLOWTAIL SNAPPER

Stripes

Whether they're vertical or horizontal, stripes can give a fish that certain something.

STRIPED MARLIN

HAWAIIAN
SQUIRRELFISH

This small fish hides in coral reefs during the day.

SHEEPSHEAD
MINNOW

ATLANTIC SPADEFISH

When they hatch, young Atlantic spadefish are black. They only become silvery gray with dark stripes as they grow up.

NORTH AMERICAN
NAKED SOLE

ATLANTIC MACKEREL

MOORISH IDOL

WAHOO

PORTUGUESE MAN-OF-WAR

Do Not Touch

Some sea creatures are best left alone. These spiky and stinging monsters can really spoil your day!

SEA ANEMONE

STINGRAY

The Portuguese man-of-war is actually a colony of hundreds of individual animals. They each do different jobs to help the colony.

A stingray uses its whip-like tail to lash out at enemies.

LIONFISH

RASCASSE

A box jellyfish's stinging tentacles can be several feet long. Their venom doesn't seem to affect sea turtles, who eat the jellyfish.

BOX JELLYFISH

STONEFISH

BLUE BANDED SEA SNAKE

Which of these creatures has the most powerful venom?

ANSWER ON PAGE 64

NORTHERN STARGAZER

The stargazer can deliver a painful electric shock.

LONG-SPINED URCHIN

Shores and Rockpools

Many creatures that live near the shore have ways of attaching themselves to rocks, so that they don't get washed away.

COMMON MUSSEL

A mussel's body produces a sticky fluid that acts like glue when it dries, and keeps the mussel firmly in place on a rock.

THREE-BARBED ROCKLING

CHITON

CALIFORNIA SHEEPSHEAD

ACORN BARNACLE

NORTHERN CLINGFISH

GREAT BLACK-BACKED GULL

The rough periwinkle is a type of small sea snail that attaches itself to shore rocks. It can survive out of water for a long time.

ROUGH PERIWINKLE

A rock goby uses its fins to cling to rocks.

ROCK GOBY

SHORE CLINGFISH

SHANNY

BATAGUR

LIMPET

HAGFISH

DIAMOND LIZARDFISH

The bummalo has huge jaws filled with sharp, curving teeth, which is uses to catch small fish and crustaceans.

Wolf herrings are large, fierce predators.

BUMMALO

One of these animals uses its sucking mouthparts to attach itself to its victim. Can you guess which one?

ANSWER ON PAGE 64

GREATER SAWFISH

WALRUS

Teeth, Tusks and Beaks

Most other creatures will give these toothy, tusky animals a wide berth.

SPERM WHALE

COMMON SAW SHARK

SEA LAMPREY

WOLF HERRING

LOGGERHEAD TURTLE

A garfish's long jaws are armed with sharp teeth.

A male narwhal has only two teeth, one of which grows into a long tusk. In rare cases, both teeth will grow into tusks.

GARFISH

NARWHAL

PIRARUCU

NATAL
GHOST FROG

The otter's webbed feet help it swim faster. It can close its nostrils and ears when it is swimming in rivers.

AMERICAN BEAVER

EURASIAN OTTER

WELS

TIGER BARB

This river dolphin is blind and uses echolocation to find food.

GANGES DOLPHIN

ANACONDA

HIPPOPOTAMUS

Of all land mammals, only elephants and rhinoceros are heavier than hippos. These massive creatures sway in the water to keep cool and come out at dusk to feed.

PLATYPUS

River Creatures

Animals of all types, from mammals to reptiles, make their homes in rivers and streams.

ARRAU RIVER TURTLE

A gharial has about 100 sharp teeth in its jaws.

WATER OPOSSUM

GHARIAL

Not So Beautiful

You could say that these creatures have a face that only a mother could love. But some of them don't even have faces!

JOHN DORY

Humpback whales "sing" to communicate with other whales.

HUMPBACK WHALE

HAMMERHEAD SHARK

Each side of a hammerhead shark's unusual head has an eye and a nostril. Scientists think this may help them see and smell more effectively.

ANGLER

BOWHEAD WHALE

Elephant seals can dive for up to two hours without taking a breath as they hunt for food. The males start developing their odd noses when they reach adulthood.

NORTHERN ELEPHANT SEAL

PINECONE FISH

BLACK SEA CUCUMBER

The sea mouse is actually a type of worm. But which creature here is related to starfish?

ANSWER ON PAGE 64

SEA MOUSE

GIANT ISOPOD

SARGASSUMFISH

The hatchetfish lives in the deep sea and glows in the dark.

BRAIN CORAL

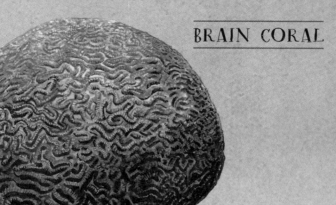

HATCHETFISH

45

Teeny Tinies

Small is beautiful when it comes to these little swimmers.

SAND EEL

DWARF SEAHORSE

This flatfish has both eyes on one side of its head.

BLACKCHEEK TONGUEFISH

PEARLFISH

ANTARCTIC KRILL

Shrimpfish are fish, not shrimp. They usually swim through the water with their heads pointing straight down.

SHRIMPFISH

PINK SHRIMP

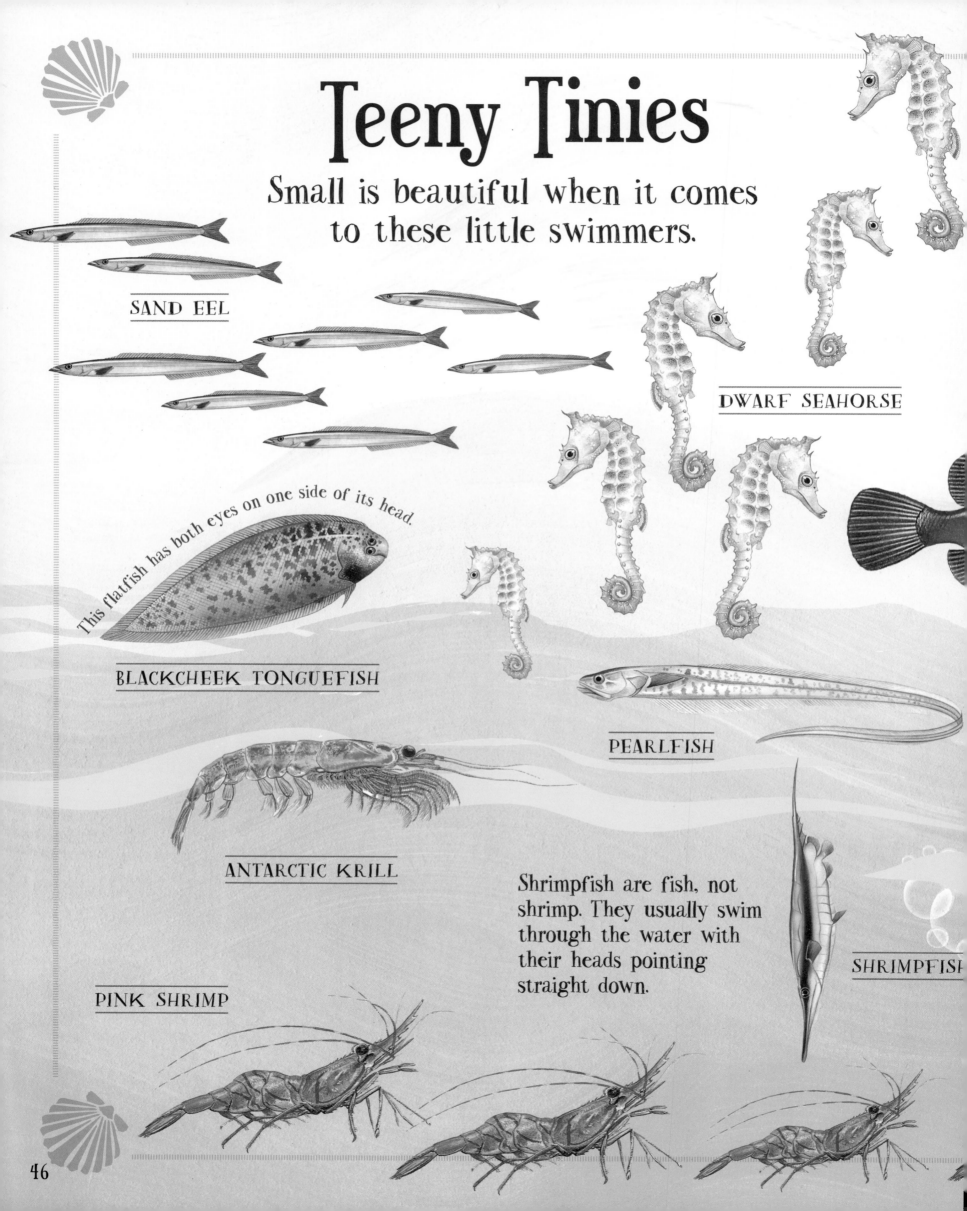

Boarfish have an extendable mouth that turns into a tube. They use it to suck up tiny worms and shrimp to eat.

RICEFISH

LESSER WEEVER

BOARFISH

LONGLURE FROGFISH

TUBESNOUT

REDLIP BLENNY

PHOTOBLEPHARON PALPEBRATUS

FIFTEENSPINE STICKLEBACK

ROSS SEAL

Ross seals are one of the smallest types of seal in Antarctica.

If any creature swimming below these harbour porpoises looks up, the porpoises' pale bellies will make them hard to see against the sunlight filtering through the water.

HARBOUR PORPOISE

MINKE WHALE

CONGER EEL

POWAN

TWAITE SHAD

BALLYHOO

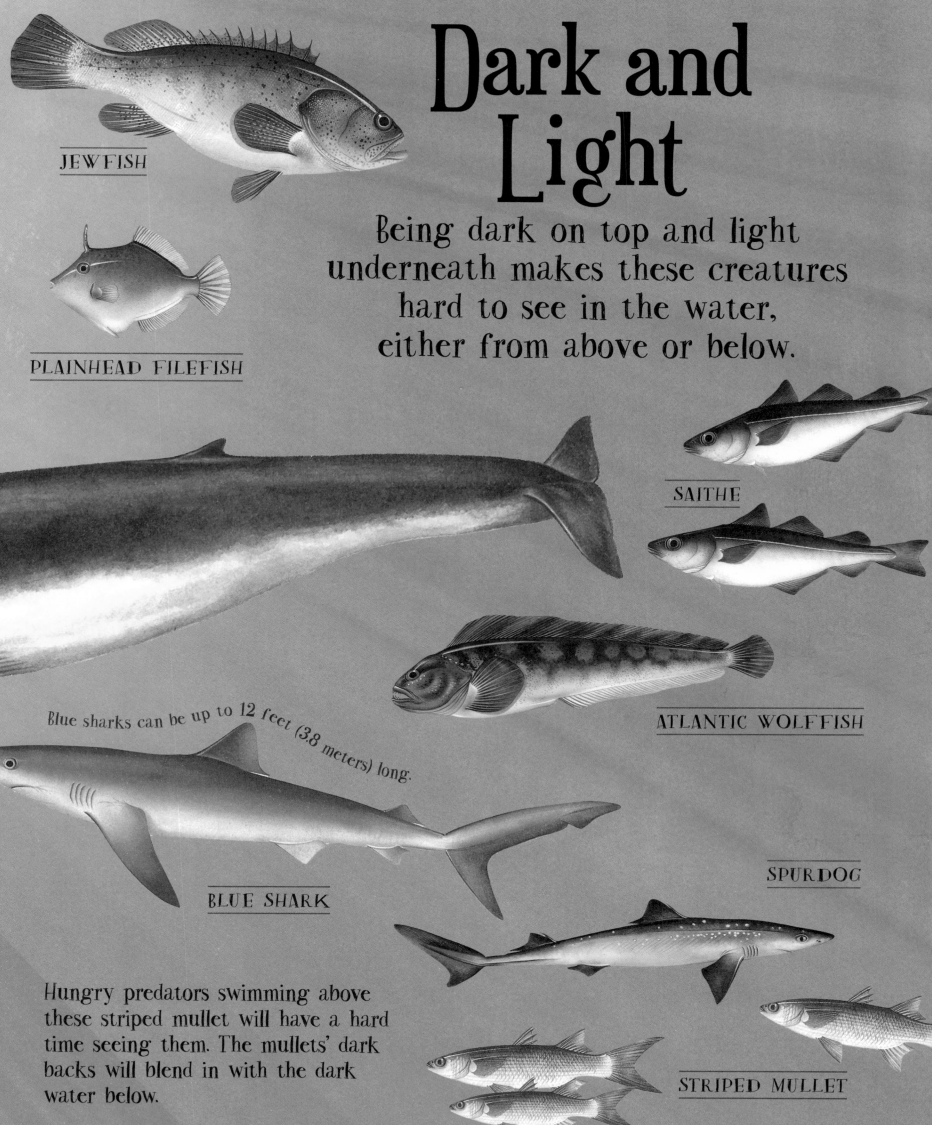

Dark and Light

Being dark on top and light underneath makes these creatures hard to see in the water, either from above or below.

JEWFISH

PLAINHEAD FILEFISH

SAITHE

ATLANTIC WOLFFISH

Blue sharks can be up to 12 feet (3.8 meters) long.

BLUE SHARK

SPURDOG

Hungry predators swimming above these striped mullet will have a hard time seeing them. The mullets' dark backs will blend in with the dark water below.

STRIPED MULLET

49

Coelacanths are sometimes referred to as "living fossils." They were thought to have been extinct for millions of years, until one was caught in 1938.

BASKING SHARK

WOLF HERRING

COELACANTH

Even though it grows up to 40 feet (12 meters) long, the whale shark eats tiny animals called plankton.

WHALE SHARK

LEATHERBACK TURTLE

Super Sized
Big is beautiful for these enormous sea creatures.

ATLANTIC MANTA

OARFISH

KILLER WHALE

Even a killer whale's fins are huge! The dorsal fin can be 6 feet (1.8 meters) tall.

A sunfish's round body can be 11 feet (3.3 meters) across. They eat mostly jellyfish and the females produce more eggs than any other fish: about 300 million at a time!

BLUEFIN TUNA

Which of these is the largest fish in the ocean?

ANSWER ON PAGE 64

OCEAN SUNFISH

51

Icefish have no hemoglobin, which is what makes other animals' blood red. Their blood looks whitish or clear.

GREENLAND SHARK

ICEFISH

ANTARCTIC COD

ARTIC CHAR

WHITE WHALE

A polar bear's thick fur helps keep it warm.

Polar Animals

These animals must not feel the cold, since they make their homes in Earth's harsh polar regions.

POLAR BEAR

ALASKA POLLOCK

Emperor penguins are the largest species of penguin. They are able to survive the harsh Antarctic winters by standing together in groups for warmth. This is also how they protect their eggs.

ADELIE PENGUIN

EMPEROR PENGUIN

Harp seals have a thick layer of insulating fat called blubber.

HARP SEAL

NORTHERN FUR SEAL

HARBOR SEAL

SNOWY SHEATHBILL

GREAT SKUA

WANDERING
ALBATROSS

Waterbirds

Not all sea creatures live in the
water. These seabirds dive or wade
into the water to find food.

ESKIMO CURLEW

The cormorant dives to catch fish,
using its webbed feet to swim. It
brings a fish to the surface and
tosses it into the air, then swallows
it headfirst.

GREAT CORMORANT

This long, strong beak can pry shellfish off rocks.

OYSTERCATCHER

PIED AVOCET

NORTHERN GANNET

GREAT FRIGATE
BIRD

Frigate birds spend most of their lives in the air.

ATLANTIC
PUFFIN

COMMON TERN

GREAT EGRET

The pelican flies high over
the ocean before making a
high-speed plunge into the
water to catch fish in the
pouch below its beak.

BROWN PELICAN

LITTLE PENGUIN

Which of these clever creatures uses tools to find food?

ANSWER ON PAGE 64

These sea lions are extremely fast swimmers.

SOUTH AMERICAN FUR SEAL

CALIFORNIA SEA LION

SEA OTTER

Despite their size, these enormous sea lions are sometimes hunted by killer whales and great white sharks.

STELLER SEA LION

HOODED SEAL

56

DUGONG

MEDITERRANEAN
MONK SEAL

Flippered Friends

These sea mammals use their strong
flippers to move through the water.

AUSTRALIAN
SEA LION

The bearded seal gets its name from the bristles on its snout.

BEARDED SEAL

If you guessed that a crabeater
seal eats crabs, you'd be wrong!
Just like blue whales, they eat tiny
shrimp-like creatures called krill.

CRABEATER SEAL

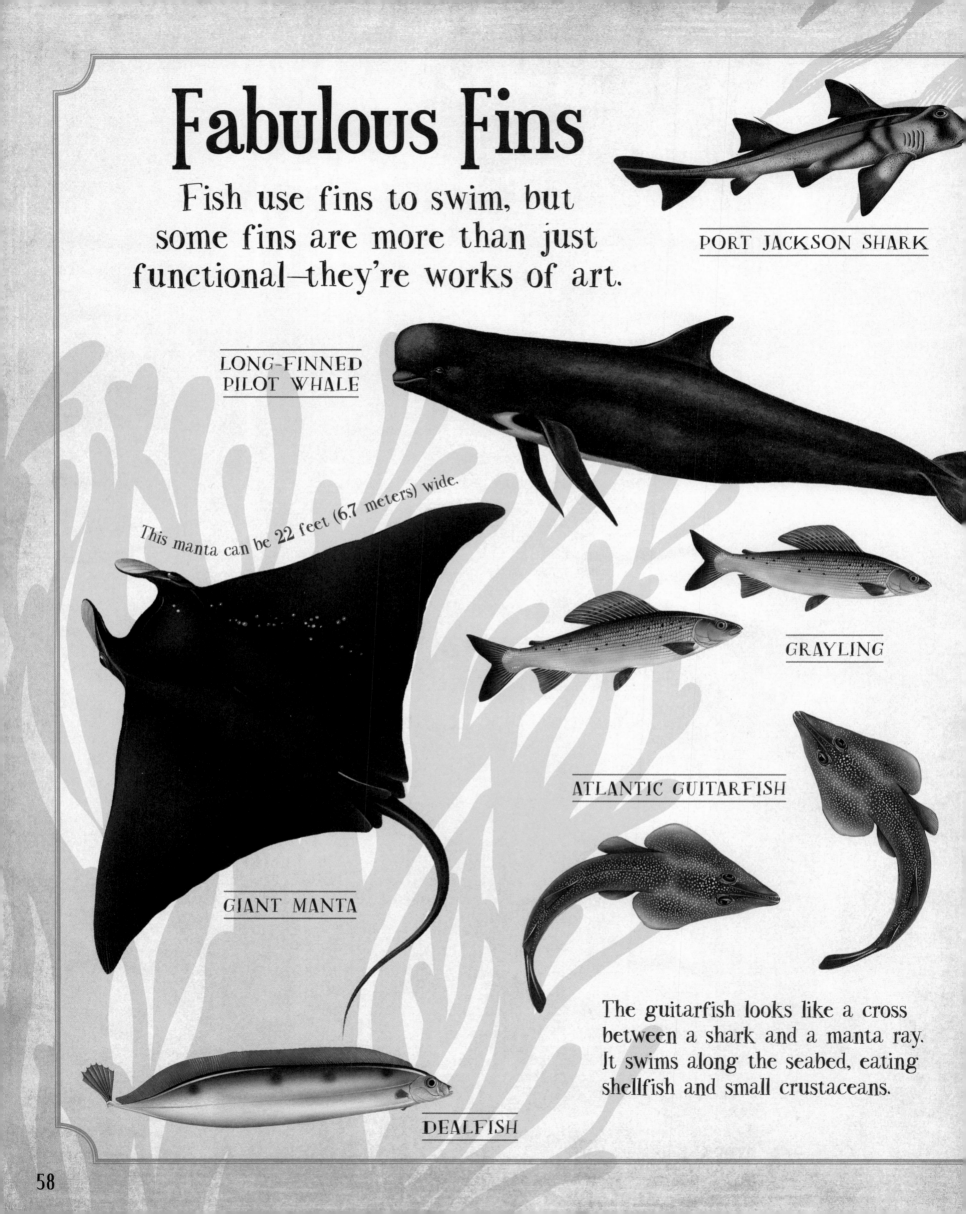

Fabulous Fins

Fish use fins to swim, but some fins are more than just functional—they're works of art.

PORT JACKSON SHARK

LONG-FINNED PILOT WHALE

This manta can be 22 feet (6.7 meters) wide.

GRAYLING

ATLANTIC GUITARFISH

GIANT MANTA

The guitarfish looks like a cross between a shark and a manta ray. It swims along the seabed, eating shellfish and small crustaceans.

DEALFISH

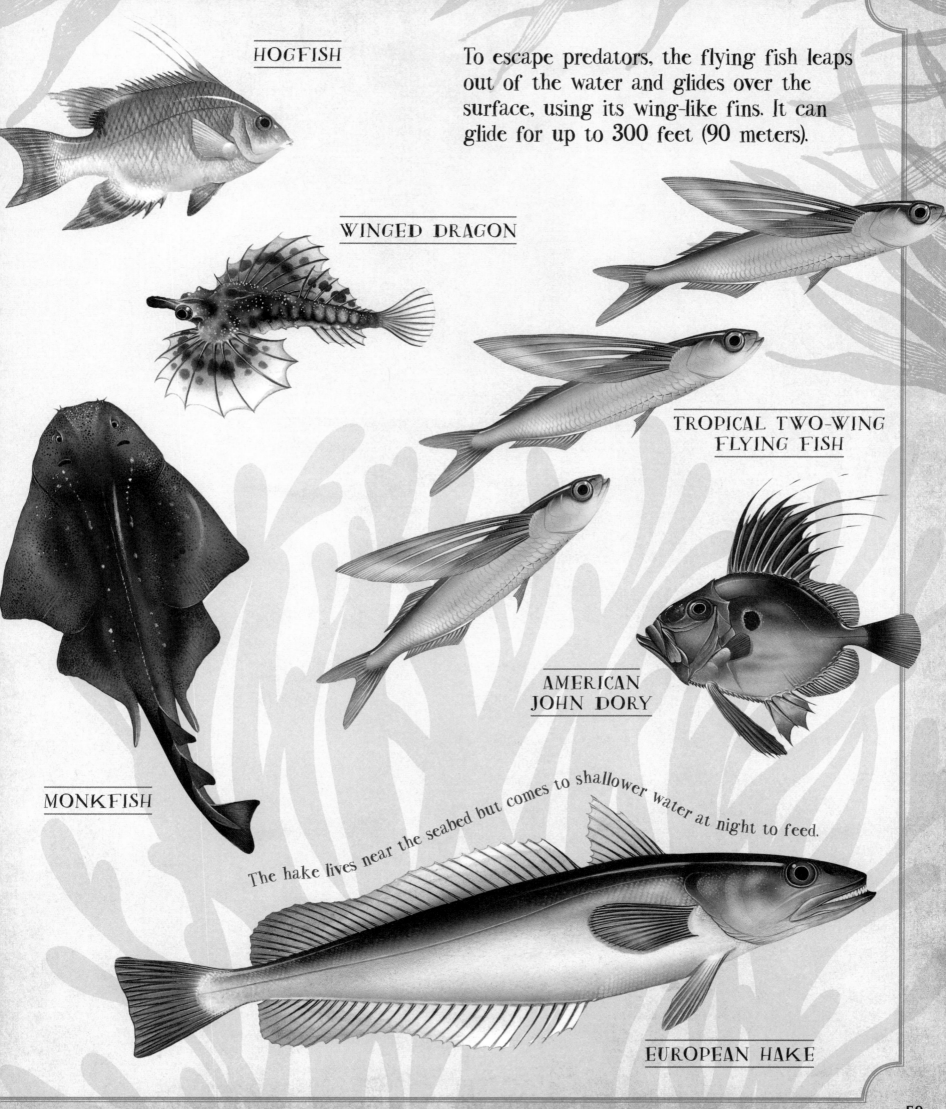

HOGFISH

To escape predators, the flying fish leaps out of the water and glides over the surface, using its wing-like fins. It can glide for up to 300 feet (90 meters).

WINGED DRAGON

TROPICAL TWO-WING FLYING FISH

AMERICAN JOHN DORY

MONKFISH

The hake lives near the seabed but comes to shallower water at night to feed.

EUROPEAN HAKE

59

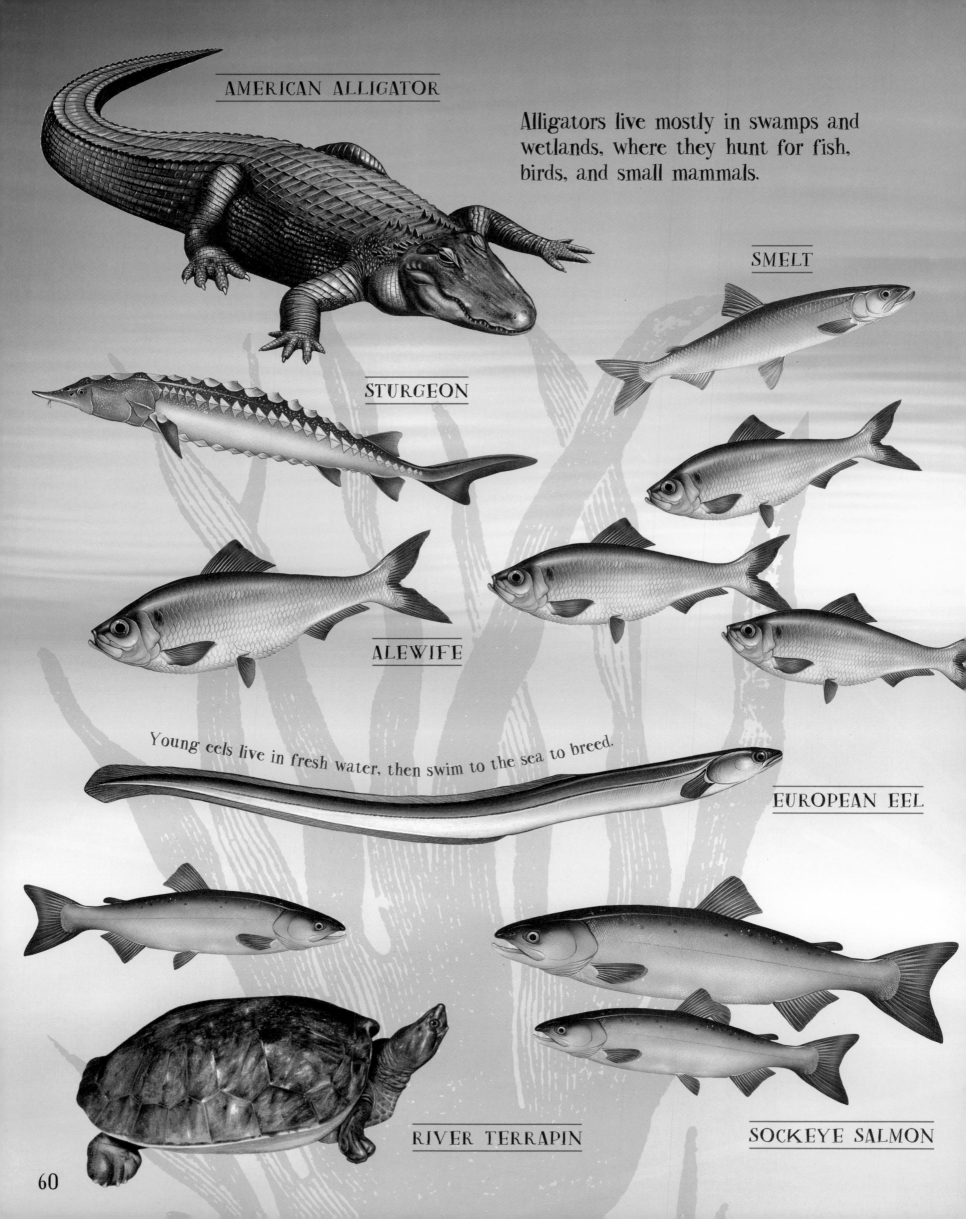

AMERICAN ALLIGATOR

Alligators live mostly in swamps and wetlands, where they hunt for fish, birds, and small mammals.

SMELT

STURGEON

ALEWIFE

Young eels live in fresh water, then swim to the sea to breed.

EUROPEAN EEL

RIVER TERRAPIN

SOCKEYE SALMON

Fresh and Salty

Rivers and lakes have fresh
water, while oceans are salty.
Some creatures are able to
live in either.

WELS

BULL SHARK

The wels is a catfish that can reach 10 feet (3 meters) in length.

Atlantic salmon hatch in freshwater,
but after a few years they swim out
to sea. They come back when it is
time to breed, usually in the same
river where they were born.

ATLANTIC SALMON

JOLLYTAIL

SPECTACLED CAIMAN

Safety In Numbers

Some fish travel in enormous groups called schools. When predators strike, it gives them a better chance of survival.

In late spring and summer, billions of sardines swim along the African coast.

Sardines are fairly small fish, about 6-12 inches (15-30 centimeters) long. They live in enormous schools, swimming along and feeding on plankton near the ocean's surface.

They are eaten in huge numbers by dolphins and sharks.

Answers

FAST SWIMMERS

Q: Which of these fish do you think is the fastest swimmer?

A: The sailfish has been clocked leaping out of the water at more than 68 miles (110 kilometers) per hour.

THE EYES HAVE IT

Q: One of these fish has spots that look like eyes, to confuse predators. Can you tell which one it is?

A: The copperband butterflyfish's large "eyespot" tricks predators into thinking that it's larger than it really is.

LAKES AND PONDS

Q: Can you find the two amphibians on these pages?

A: The axolotl and the marsh frog are both amphibians. Axolotls are a type of salamander.

CORAL REEFS

Q: Which of these reef fish has an armored body for protection?

A: Joined plates make a hard shell around the yellow boxfish's body. The only breaks in the armor are the mouth, eyes, fins, and gills.

FIERCE PREDATORS

Q: Which of these hunters tips seals off of ice floes to catch them?

A: Killer whales have been spotted swimming under ice floes to tip seals into the water, where they can be caught.

DO NOT TOUCH

Q: Which of these creatures has the most powerful venom?

A: The box jellyfish has the second-most-powerful venom in the animal world. Its sting can easily kill a person.

TEETH, TUSKS & BEAKS

Q: One of these animals uses its sucking mouthparts to attach itself to its victim. Can you guess which one?

A: The sea lamprey sucks blood by using its circular, toothed mouth to attach to another animal's body.

NOT SO BEAUTIFUL

Q: The sea mouse is actually a type of worm. But which creature here is related to starfish?

A: The sea cucumber may be long and thin, but it's still related to starfish.

SUPER SIZED

Q: Which of these is the largest fish in the ocean?

A: The whale shark is the world's largest fish, but it's a gentle giant.

FLIPPERED FRIENDS

Q: Which of these clever creatures uses tools to find food?

A: The sea otter floats on its back with a rock on its chest, then smashes clams against the rock to open them.